IN YOUTH WE
LEARN
In Age We Understand
A Life Manual

REV. MARY B. REINERT

ISBN 978-1-64114-703-3 (paperback)
ISBN 978-1-64114-704-0 (digital)

Christian Faith Publishing, Inc.
832 Park Avenue
Meadville, PA 16335
www.christianfaithpublishing.com

Printed in the United States of America

DEDICATION

This manual is dedicated to the generations yet to come. It is my hope that you can learn from other people's experiences. You need not walk alone.

THE FAMILY TREE

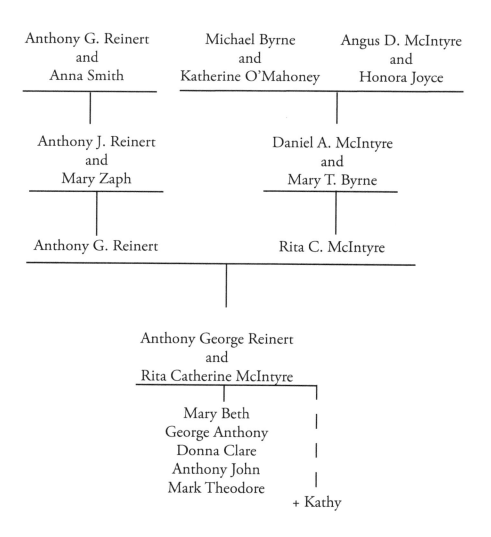

Anthony G. Reinert
and
Anna Smith

Michael Byrne
and
Katherine O'Mahoney

Angus D. McIntyre
and
Honora Joyce

Anthony J. Reinert
and
Mary Zaph

Daniel A. McIntyre
and
Mary T. Byrne

Anthony G. Reinert

Rita C. McIntyre

Anthony George Reinert
and
Rita Catherine McIntyre

Mary Beth
George Anthony
Donna Clare
Anthony John
Mark Theodore

+ Kathy

TOO SOON OLD,
TOO LATE SMART

When I started writing this manual (this is my third attempt), I thought that I might be able to pass along some meaningful information and thereby save future generations from needless mistakes. Now I believe we all have to make the mistakes for ourselves, even if it means making the same mistakes in multiple generations.

What I've discovered is that the wisdom I now know in my heart I knew years ago in my head. I now know that the most significant journey we make in our lifetime is in the eighteen-inch distance we travel from our head to our heart.

There are, however, three pieces of advice I want to pass along:

1. Don't ever love or want someone or something so much that you can't walk away if the deal goes bad. Know your deal breakers before you begin the deal, and always remember that you are the only one to reach the conclusion to break the deal.

2. When someone tells you who they are, believe them! And, believe them the first time they tell you. What I mean is this: the first time someone tells you a lie, they are a liar; the first time someone steals, they are a thief; and the first time someone is abusive (mentally, emotionally, physically), they are an abuser.

3. Live a simple life. Now don't go crazy and turn Amish. That is not what I mean. But I do mean return to basics, live below your means, and enjoy the magic that you find in the ordinary progression of ordinary days.

That's all, folks.

I PRAY

For years now, every morning, I have prayed the Ninety-First Psalm over each and every one of you. So from now into eternity:

Psalm 91
You who dwell in the shelter of the Most High, who
abide in the shadow of the Almighty, say to the Lord, My
refuge and my fortress, my God, in whom I trust.
For He will rescue you from the snare of the fowler, from
the destroying pestilence, with His pinions he will cover
you, and under His wings you shall take refuge,
His faithfulness is a buckler and a shield.
You shall not fear the terror of the night nor the arrow
that flies by day; not the pestilence that roams in
darkness nor the devastating plague at noon.
Though a thousand fall at your side, ten thousand
at your right side, near you it shall not come.
Rather with your eyes shall you behold and
see the requital of the wicked.
Because you have made the Lord your refuge; you have
made the Most High your stronghold, no evil shall befall
you nor shall affliction come near your tent.
For to His angels He has given command about you that
they shall guard you in all your ways; upon their hands they
shall bear you up lest you dash your foot against a stone.

You shall tread upon the asp and the viper; you shall
trample down the lion and the dragon.
Because he clings to me, I will deliver him;
I will set him on high because he acknowledges my name.
He shall call upon me, and I will answer him
and I will be with him in distress;
I will deliver him and glorify him; with length of days I
will gratify him and I will show him my salvation

Oh, for those of you who are wondering, this is the Catholic version.

WARNING

The opinions expressed in this document are strictly those of the author and, therefore, are not subject to debate.

For additional insight and guidance, read on, but read at your own risk.

CONTENTS

ACKNOWLEDGEMENTS

To the generations that have gone before me: your strength, your courage, your commitment, your love lives on and grows. Thank you.

To Jan and George and Meg, who contributed to this manual, and to all those who supported and encouraged me in this effort. Thank you.

To Anthony, who asked the questions, pushed my buttons, and pressured me enough to write this manual: I hope this provides the answers and guidance you were looking for. You have no idea of the journey you sent me on. Thank You.

To my editing staff: Amy, Chris, Gus, and Robyn—for your reviews, comments, and corrections. I appreciate all you've done. I'm blessed to have you in my life. Thank you.

PART I

Thoughts and Reflections

*Trust God from the bottom of your heart; don't
try to figure out everything on your own.
Listen for God's voice in everything you do; everywhere you go,
He's the one who will keep you on track.
Don't assume that you know it all.
Run to God! Run from evil!
Your body will glow with health; your very bones will vibrate with life!
Honor God with everything you own.
Give him the first and the best.
Your barns will burst.
Your wine vats will brim over.
But don't, dear friend, resent God's discipline;
don't sulk under his loving correction.
It's the child He loves that God corrects; a father's
delight is behind all this. (Proverbs 3:5–12)*

AGE * MATURITY * LIFE STAGES

"It's through me, Lady Wisdom, that your life deepens, and the years of your life ripen. Live wisely and wisdom will permeate your life; mock life and life will mock you."

—Proverbs 9:11–12

Age is an interesting concept. After all, if you live long enough, you grow old. You don't necessarily mature, but you do physically grow older.

When we're very young, we mark our time in months, then years, and even half years (three and a half, four and a half, etc.). We rush the years because we just can't wait to be old enough to (fill in the blank). We're either too young or too old for everything.

Once we hit the double digits, the half years disappear and we count the time to sixteen, when we'll be old enough to drive; eighteen, when we're old enough to vote, and the big one, twenty-one, when we're old enough to drink. Upon reaching twenty-one, the "age of maturity," we start fearing growing old; after all, thirty is just around the corner.

The thirties, forties, and fifties—yes, we approach each of these decades with more trepidation, dread, and, yes, fear of growing old. This is a time for a lot more responsibility, more painful growth and experience, a time for building for ourselves and for our families.

19

Then one day, we arrive at sixty, and we realize it's our time and that all this growth and experience equals freedom.

You're neither too young nor too old. There's no one to impress. You've accumulated the experience, the education, the time, the money, and the freedom to discover and explore the person you are meant to be. You're accountable to yourself for yourself.

Then suddenly, you wake up one morning and you're eighty-nine and a half years old. People have decided to agree to disagree with you. They no longer debate or negotiate with you; they simply accept your behavior. And so you have arrived, and along the way, you've passed through aging, to maturity, to acceptance.

There seem to be twelve stages in life that each and every one of us passes through. Here they are and, in my opinion, with the one word that is the embodiment of each stage:

1. Prebirth: Potential
2. Birth: Hope
3. Infancy: Vitality
4. Early childhood: Playfulness
5. Middle childhood: Imagination
6. Late childhood: Ingenuity
7. Adolescence: Passion
8. Early adulthood: Enterprise
9. Midlife: Contemplation
10. Mature adulthood: Benevolence
11. Late adulthood: Wisdom
12. Death and dying: Life

Think about it!

AGE * MATURITY * LIFE STAGES

THE SECRET

Experience, enjoy, and celebrate each stage along the way.

OUR GOAL

Not to arrive at death's door well-preserved and in pristine condition but rather to slide into the grave bruised, scarred, healed, worn out, and totally spent from having wholly lived your life.

BUSINESS

"A thick bankroll is no help when life falls apart; but a
principled life can stand up to the worst."

—Proverbs 11:4

The concept of business enters into every area of our lives. Life
requires the development of basic management skills. Business is 90
percent generic and 10 percent specific. Whether your business is
retail, wholesale, professional, blue collar, health care, personal ser-
vices, or product oriented, you must apply the same business management skills, or you will not survive.

As always, the choice is yours. If what you love and enjoy and
want to spend your life doing is that 10 percent that is specific, then
take a job. You'll report to a boss, but you won't have ultimate responsibility. There is always someone higher up to pass the blame to. Get
up in the morning, and put your full energy into that job. Work
hard, be loyal, and leave the job behind you when you go home.
You'll spend your work life doing the thing you enjoy.

If what gets your juices moving is management and owning an
operation, then open a business. It doesn't matter what you go into,
but it should be something that you know, understand, and are capa-
ble of doing. It should not be something that you want to do every
day of your life.

If your business is to first survive and then thrive, you will spend
most of your time exercising your management skills. You will need
to envision, forecast, budget, account, market, purchase, sell, and

employ. If you're doing the 10 percent that is specific to your business, you are not doing your job. Mismanagement will quickly turn the American dream into a nightmare.

A common misconception about being in business for yourself is that you don't have a boss. The fact is you answer to your customers, your employees, your vendors, and the government. That's right, you have all those hoops to jump through. The difference is that you get to decide whose hoops and when you've had enough.

There is a middle ground. It's self-employment. This is where you get to do everything, both the 10 percent specific that you enjoy doing and are good at and the 90 percent generic that's necessary to succeed in business. The problem with self-employment is that you limit your growth to how much you are able to physically, emotionally, financially, creatively, and productively handle. It is a major balancing act because you are never able to separate who you are from what you do. It is, however, the area where you dance to your own music in that you are your own boss and don't have employees.

Let's carry this concept one step further. You need to employ all these business skills to the management of your life. Goal setting and decision making are at the core of an organized life, a managed life, a disciplined life. You set the goal. You create the plan. You define success.

BUSINESS

THE SECRET

There is no secret here; management and discipline are the keys.

OUR GOAL

To manage your life to meet your definition of success.

CHILDREN * PARENTS

"Pay close attention, friend, to what your father tells you; never forget what you learn at your mother's knee."

—Proverbs 1:8

Children do not belong to their parents; they come through their parents but belong to God. God places them with specific parents and entrusts those parents with that child's care and development.

Parents owe their children two things: roots and wings. Each set of parents will develop their own style, but they must remember that it is not the job of the parent to be their child's best friend; it is their responsibility to parent. Now that's a tightrope walk.

Parents, you need to develop a close working and walking relationship with your children. Become intimately involved in the day-to-day lives of your children, but never forget that you are the parent and they are the children. This starts by setting an example and establishing the character and value system for your family. Children are always watching the most important people in their lives, and the best teachers teach by example. Kids catch so much more than they are taught.

Parents need to work side by side with their children to discover their interests and talents—encouraging, directing, guiding their lives. Always be alert to teachable moments. Lovingly introduce your children to quality stewardship. Teach your children self-discipline, the difference between wants and needs, and how to make good choices. Teach them to manage their lives. Teach them to think, to plan, to organize.

Parents, your first goal is to do better by your children than you got. This is not to blame our parents for the way they raised us. You can't teach what you don't know. This is about growth and progress and paying it forward.

Parents, if you have succeeded in creating a positive, open working relationship with your children, then there should never be a need to have the big sit-down talk (about drugs, friends, sex, work, etc.). You should be able to bring these conversations up or allow your child to address these questions over many years of talking honestly and openly with your child. This starts at birth and ends at death. If they are old enough to ask (whatever), they deserve a straightforward, age-appropriate, honest answer.

Your child should never be afraid to talk with you or call on you for or about anything. They should be able to pick up the phone and know it doesn't matter if they're stoned or drunk or locked up—you're there for them. Tough love comes the morning after. They should know that even if you are disappointed and disapprove of their choices, you still love them and you have their back.

Now, after spending years raising children to be functional adults, set them free. It is now time to become their best friend and confidant.

Thoughts from Aunt Jan and Uncle George

You may be surprised to discover that your natural tendency is to become your parents. It will surprise you when your parents' words come out of your mouth. This is the way life goes. Be comfortable growing into your own person, and be accepting of the wisdom of your parents.

CHILDREN * PARENTS

THE SECRET

Open communication, honesty, and love.

OUR GOAL

To live long enough to forgive your parents for
the mistakes you believe they made.

CONSUMER CREDIT

"Dear friend, if you've gone into hock with your neighbor or locked yourself into a deal with a stranger, if you've impulsively promised the shirt off your back and now find yourself shivering out in the cold, friend don't waste a minute, get yourself out of that mess."

—Proverbs 6:1–2

Despite popular belief, there is no such thing as "good credit." Consumer credit is a slippery slope no matter where you get onboard.

I can hear you all now: "But what about my FICO score? I need credit to buy a house. I can't book an airplane flight, or a hotel room, or rent a car without a credit card." That's all wrong!

A FICO score has nothing to do with your ability to deal with finances and everything to do with your relationship to debt. That's right, it's about your relationship to debt, and all debt is bad.

As for needing a credit card, a debit card from your bank dealing in cash is every bit as functional as a credit card. Most people when deciding whether they can afford something ask themselves, "Can I afford the payment?" The real question should be, "Do I have the cash?" Guess what, when you deal in cash, you just got an 18 percent a year increase in purchasing power.

As for a mortgage, with enough of a down payment, you can get a fifteen-year mortgage without a FICO score (if you know where). Mortgages, as we know them, did not exist in this country until after World War I. Prior to that, people would come up with a down payment, then make regular payments and, after a number of years, one balloon payment. It was not unusual for people to pay cash for their homes.

Our great-great-grandfather, Mike Byrne, was a butcher in the "yards." He used to walk back and forth to work from his home on Forty-Sixth and Marshfield. He would follow the trolley tracks and picked up the change that jiggled loose from the conductors' change holder. This was his second job. He used that change to pay cash for the new brick bungalow he had built at Sixty-Second and Fairfield.

Thoughts from Aunt Jan and Uncle George

Be cautious about consumer credit as it makes you the slave if not used appropriately. Using credit carelessly can put you in debt. It is satisfying to purchase the things you want; just please pay your bill in full each month.

Familiarize yourself with the advice of Dave Ramsey, and limit your debt so you don't have to work harder and longer to make ends meet. Consumer credit (debt) can be the number one enemy to building your wealth.

CONSUMER CREDIT

THE SECRET

Don't fall prey to the credit trap.

OUR GOAL

To overcome debt by staying far away from credit.

DATING

"Escape quickly from the company of fools; they're a
waste of your time, a waste of your words."
—Proverbs 14:7

Now here's an interesting topic. Dating is all about having fun;
exploring your interests, your likes and dislikes; and trying on other
single people to see how they fit.

I really like the idea of "safe dating," where you hang out with a
large group of your friends and do things together in groups. Dating
is about you. It's about going places and doing things you like with
lots of people you're attracted to. Dating is about developing relationship skills.

By the time you start breaking down into couples, you should
have made a decision on whether you're planning on getting married
or staying single. If you're getting married, it's time to stop dating
and start courting.

Dating is about the search. Courting is about the commitment.

Dating is off-the-rack shopping. Dating is trying on many
single people to see if they fit. Once you find a custom fit, dating
becomes courting. Courting comes after you believe you have found
the one person you intend to marry.

While courting, you continue having fun and matching your
likes and interests but expand your exploration into the more
important areas of matching your character and values as well as
your goals and dreams. Courting is about finding that one person to

partner with for the rest of your life. The goal is a lifelong committed marriage.

It's not enough to love this person. Each of you will fall in and out and back into love. This must be a person you really like. This has to be someone you can laugh with, play with, as well as dream and plan with. This person has to be the one who will hold you accountable for your actions, the person who will inspire and motivate you. This is not one-sided; it works both ways. The two of you will walk through life leaning against each other so that neither of you will fall down.

DATING

THE SECRET

You're looking for custom made in an off-the-rack world.

THE GOAL

To find the one person in the world who is completely opposite of you yet is in total agreement with you, then spend your life balancing each other.

DECISIONS

"I am Lady Wisdom, and I live next to Sanity;
Knowledge and Discretion live just down the street."
—Proverbs 8:12

In our lifetimes, we make hundreds of thousands of decisions. Three of these are major and important decisions:

1. To choose Christ as your personal Lord and Savior.
2. The person you choose to marry or partner with for the rest of your life.
3. What you want your life to say about who you are/were.

These decisions will direct the balance of your life. You make a fundamental decision to choose good over evil, right over wrong, positive over negative, and your life is off and running. Every other decision you will make in your life is minor, flexible, and subject to that fundamental decision that you've already made.

Some of these decisions will be big and some will be small. Where do I want to live or work? Do I want to have children? Do I want oatmeal or Cheerios? Do we buy a new car? Do we go on vacation? Should I wear black or navy blue?

Some of these decisions will become routine and others will always require analysis, consideration, education, and research. Don't allow the research process to freeze the decision making process.

Ultimately, you will find a decision model that works for you. Some methods I've used are to list positives versus negatives using a steno pad (the line down the middle of the page gives you a quick overview). I try to look at the situation as if it were being played out on the evening news, or I ask myself, "What's the worst thing that can happen, and can I live with that?" I use the standard bell curve a lot in my life.

The more decisions you make, the better you get at making decisions. If the decision you make turns out wrong, guess what? You get to make another decision. More practice!

Thoughts from Aunt Jan and Uncle George

Your best decisions are the ones you make after you have weighed the pros and cons and find it feels right. Poor decisions are often made quickly or without sufficient thought. Do not allow others to pressure you when making a decision. Give yourself time to think things through.

Have you ever heard the saying "Let me sleep on that"? Not only does that give you the time and space to think it through but also it allows the answers to come to you while you are relaxed.

Please make decisions and take action upon your decisions; not doing so creates a stagnant life. Don't worry about making the wrong decision (as long as you truly believe in your decision) as life is about the journey, trying things, and learning. You can always make a new decision in another direction if that suits you.

DECISIONS

THE SECRET

Don't allow analysis paralysis to take hold.

OUR GOAL

Make choices. Don't let life just happen to you.

DISCIPLINE

"So, my dear friends listen carefully; those who embrace these my ways are most blessed. Mark a life of discipline and live wisely; don't squander your precious life."

—Proverbs 8:32–33

The first thing we need to get our heads around is that discipline is far more than mere punishment. Imposed discipline brought on you by outside authority can and often is viewed as mere punishment. However, even discipline for the sheer sake of discipline, when it is self-discipline, has merit. The practice of discipline leads to an ordered life.

Discipline does not mean living a limited or restrictive life. Discipline does not mean giving up what you enjoy or relinquishing fun and recreation. Now that we know what discipline is not, let's talk about self-discipline.

Self-discipline is the voice inside your head directing your life. It is the ability to control your impulses, emotions, and behavior. It is being able to turn down instant gratification in favor of gaining the long-term satisfaction and fulfillment from achieving higher and more meaningful goals. To possess self-discipline is to be able to make decisions, take action, and execute your game plan regardless of the obstacles, the discomfort, or difficulties that may come your way.

While we struggle against imposed discipline, self-discipline is actual freedom. Parents, your lives will be easier if you involve your children in the process of setting up their routines. Self-discipline is about order and choice. To live without discipline is to trade order for chaos. To live without discipline is to live your life in the impulse of the moment and to doom yourself to overreacting in life situations and repeating past mistakes.

The *self* in self-discipline makes all the difference. The *self* makes it your choice; you establish your standards of behavior. This is really important since living a disciplined life requires the exercise of self-control. Just like making decisions, the more you practice self-control, the better you get at it and, ultimately, the easier life becomes.

When you live a self-disciplined life, you create order, stay organized, set up personal systems, stay efficient, and structure your time and physical space. Living a self-disciplined life means learning to focus your mind and energy on your goals and persevere until you achieve them. This is cultivating a mind-set whereby you rule your life by deliberate choices and not by your emotions, bad habits, or peer pressure.

To achieve self-discipline, start with baby steps. Figure out what motivates you and what your bad triggers are. Develop strategies to avoid or overpower your triggers. Make your behavior as routine as possible. Practice self-denial, and use sports and exercise to escape. Identify what inspires you, and visualize your reward.

DISCIPLINE

THE SECRET

At the core of self-discipline is feeling good
and being well satisfied with your life.

OUR GOAL

To pursue your dreams and goals through order and structure.

DREAMS

"It pays to take life seriously; things work out when you trust in God."

—Proverbs 16:20

I'm not talking about the dreams we have at night when we're sleeping. I'm talking about the dream God put inside you, that one that is so much at the core of your being that you don't dare share it with others and is so big that only God could make it happen. So let me tell you a story.

Once upon a time, a young Mike Byrne (a man who just happens to be my great-grandfather), just ahead of the constable, jumped aboard a ship, stowed away, and landed in Canada.

Now what you have to understand is at this time in Ireland Catholics were not allowed to practice their faith, to own land or businesses, to go to school, or even to know how to read or write. Not unlike being a slave in the South before emancipation. Mike, however, could read, write, and count because he had attended the illegal hedge schools. He was absolutely certain, as only a hard-headed Irishman could be certain, about two things in life. Down deep inside he knew the place was America and the answer was education.

Mike eventually made his way to Chicago, got married, and had ten children. Four died in infancy or preschool age, but the other six all finished grade school, and some went to high school. Of his grandchildren, all finished high school and some went on to college. (He lived to see this.) Most of his great-grandchildren have some college, many have degrees, and some have advanced degrees. His great-great-grandchildren (your generation) have grown up understanding that college is the baseline measurement and is expected.

Thoughts from Aunt Jan and Uncle George

Always dream; don't allow anyone to dampen your dreams. Dreams become reality when you get up and work toward them. Dreams may change or modify. Dreams die when you quit chasing them.

Dream about things that are important to you, and work toward your dreams. You really can make your dreams come true.

DREAMS

THE SECRET

Stay focused. It may take three to four generations
for you to see that great dream come true.

OUR GOAL

Never stop believing in the dream God put in your heart. Keep
moving forward. God is a faithful God, and it will come to pass.

EDUCATION

"The wise accumulate knowledge a true treasure; know-it-alls talk too much-a sheer waste."

—Proverbs 10:14

Contrary to popular belief, the majority of our education does not take place in school. Our first and primary education begins with the family, and it starts the moment you're born.

Parents, beware: most of this education comes from observation and modeling, and it takes place when you're not watching.

We draw our self-worth and value from the primary people in our lives. These are our parents, our siblings, and our extended family. The best teachers teach by example. We need to teach our children to think, to plan, to organize. This is the way we do things in our family.

The family is where we learn what is and is not acceptable behavior. This may or may not be the way the rest of the world functions, but it is the way we operate. The family is where we learn how to treat other people, how to interact in society, where we learn right from wrong and establish our moral compass. Although this family education is ongoing, taking place throughout our lifetime, most of the foundation work is in place before we go off to school.

School is the formal part of our education. There was a time when eight years of elementary school was enough. Then came a time when a high school diploma would be entry into a decent life.

Now a four-year college degree is the basic entry level. This is twelve years of learning the right answers to a set of questions that simply must be endured, and then four years of massaging your thinking so that you can present it in a form that is acceptable as established answers to life's problems.

This is where we learn how to make our way in the world, where we get the fundamental tools we need to provide for ourselves and our families in our adult lives. This is where you'll make contacts that will start you on your life's path and carry with you all your life.

And now the greatest educator of all: life!

This is where you get to put it all together. This is where you discover your strengths and weaknesses. This is where you get to be all that you can be. This is where you get to take everything you've learned and mold it, and tweak it, and massage it, and reformat it, and present yourself to the world as the unique, one-and-only person you were designed to be.

Do life from a position of love, of strength, of integrity. You'll slip and stumble and fall, but you keep on learning. It may take some time to rebound, to get back up, to dust yourself off, but if you keep getting up, you will keep moving forward. You'll learn from every mistake and be better for it.

Thoughts from Aunt Jan and Uncle George

Education is your ticket to the world. Continual learning keeps you alive, relevant, and young. Knowledge comes from many sources all around you.

Try to learn from those around you. It might be easier to learn from the mistakes of others than to repeat them.

Thoughts from Aunt Meg

If you're going to make a mistake in life, make it FABULOUSLY. That way, the lesson you learn will stick, and you won't ever have to make that mistake again.

EDUCATION

THE SECRET

We learn by example. We teach by example.
When you stop learning, you start to die.

OUR GOAL

Don't ever be less than the special one of a kind
masterpiece that God created you to be.

EMOTIONS

"Truth lasts; lies are here today, gone tomorrow."
—Proverbs 12:19

We grew up in an environment that refused to acknowledge emotions. I think we were too busy surviving to allow emotions to enter into whatever circumstance we needed to deal with. In looking back, we did what we needed to do, but I think there is a better way to do life.

Emotions are real, positive, negative, and worthy of respect. They set us up for the best and worst experiences of our lives. We need to pay attention to our emotions but not let them rule our lives.

We need to acknowledge, embrace, and analyze the emotions in our lives. Don't force them down and ignore them. Years from now, when you least expect it, these emotions will come back and bite you in the _____ butt.

The positive emotions will thrust us forward and guide us. The negative emotions will set off red flags to protect us. All emotions are good and serve a purpose. Due diligence is the answer.

We need to analyze our emotions, figure out what's driving them, and then use them in our lives in a positive way. Don't wallow in the negative emotions. Give the negative emotions your full attention for about fifteen minutes, then put them aside and do something positive, come to a conclusion, and move on. You can always revisit them; they have a way of showing up again and again.

EMOTIONS

THE SECRET

Stay in touch with your inner self.

OUR GOAL

To live a balanced life.

EXPERIENCE

"If you love learning, you love discipline that goes
with it—how shortsighted to refuse correction!"
—Proverbs 12:1

Life is the experience, and experience is the greatest of educations.

I think experience is everything that ever happens in your life. Some experiences are good, some are not so good, and still others are downright bad; but all of it is life altering.

Experience is joyful. Experience is passionate. Experience is motivating. Experience is painful. Experience is happy and sad. Experience is challenge and achievement.

Experience is cumulative. When experiences get mixed together, they create our character, our values, our moral compass, our sense of humor, our dreams, even our choice of career. Our life experiences come from and impact every area of our life.

You know how sometimes you just get a feeling? Well, that gut feeling is based in your life experiences. Pay attention to it. Good judgment is found in past experience, and past experience is often based in bad judgment. Your greatest lessons are the mistakes of your past.

We carry our life experiences with us. Any two of us, side by side, in the same situation are not having the same experience because we bring with us the baggage of our own personal history. Learn from your life experiences, and use those experiences to create your own future. Those situations of your past have a way of coming back around until you learn the lesson they're intent on teaching you.

Life is the experience, and where you are on the ride is exactly where you're supposed to be. Embrace the experience. Enjoy the experience. Learn from the experience. Life as you experience it is all meant for your good.

EXPERIENCE

THE SECRET

Every single day is a brand-new life experience; embrace it!

THE GOAL

Live! Live! Live! "Life is a banquet, and
most poor bastards are starving."

FAMILY

"Friends love through all kinds of weather, and families stick together in all kinds of trouble."
—Proverbs 17:17

It's Christmas Eve, and the family has gathered in Lake Forest. As tradition has it, we've lit the Christmas candle and placed it in the window. We're going around the room, each of us taking our turn with the Christmas toast.

This year, Anthony's friend and roommate Yuri is spending the holiday with us. He takes the cup to toast and tells us that he's been in the States for six years and will be returning to Russia after the first of the year. He'll probably never be able to come back to the United States.

He tells us how good it is to spend the holiday, for the first time, with a "normal" family. Spontaneously, there was a chorus of, "Oh, this is not normal."

That's right. We are not normal. We know it, and we're proud of it. The more exposure you have to other families, the more you will come to realize and appreciate that our family is unique. Our family is a collection of people who actually like each other and just happen to be related by blood. We recognize that we are special and accept the responsibility to maintain and protect our uniqueness.

The family you're in was specially selected for you by a very personal God. He places so much importance on the family that He actually created the family before He created His church. In selecting your family, God considered the journey you're on and the lessons you need to learn, and then placed you in exactly the circumstances you needed to complete His mission for your life.

The family is the first society to embrace a child. It is the primary responsibility of the parents, backed up by the extended family, to raise the child up. "Raised up" is so much more than growing up. It's the family that will educate, discipline, prepare and introduce you to the world. It's the family's job to ensure that you become the individual that God created you to be. This is where our family excels.

The more there are positive adults who are involved in a child's life, the better off that child is. In our family, we raise up unique individuals who not only love each other but also actually like each other. We celebrate our individuality while we support and encourage each other even when we don't fully understand. We do our own thing, and we have each other's backs.

We're a strong family. I attribute much of this strength to the longevity of our marriages and the stability that flows from those partnerships. We respect each other. We really only have two traditional events each year, Christmas Eve and the family reunion. We don't just keep our traditions but rather our traditions keep us together. Finally, we help each other whenever it's necessary.

Often, when people talk about strength, they use the mighty oak tree as an example. When I think of the strength of our family, I think of the willow tree. When the storm comes and the wind blows, the oak often breaks under the stress of inflexibility, but the willow will bend, sway, give, and then spring back.

We draw strength from each other. Our strength is in the level of commitment we make to our marriages, to our families, to ourselves, and to each other. We weather the storms together and come through those storms better off than we were before.

Thoughts from Aunt Jan and Uncle George

Your family will be there for you no matter what happens, no matter where you are in life. Always love, trust, and forgive your family. Love your family, especially in the difficult times. Cherish your family always.

FAMILY

THE SECRET

Great-grandfather Dan McIntyre's dying
word to his family: "Cooperate."

OUR GOAL

Remember who you are, and choose your partners well.

FINANCE

"The poor are always ruled over by the rich; so don't
borrow and put yourself under their power."
—Proverbs 22:7

There are two worlds of finance. The first is Kingdom Finance and refers to the way we look at money through spiritual eyes. The second is World Finance and refers to how the world relates to money.

The only place in the Bible where God invites us to test Him is in reference to the tithe; money is the second most discussed topic in the Bible. The tithe (for those of us from a Catholic background) refers to giving the first 10 percent of the fruits of your efforts to the work of God's church.

Now, 10 percent, from the perspective of the world, that's a lot of money. But when you look at 10 percent from God's perspective, you see everything belongs to God, and He's letting us keep 90 percent of His stuff. That sounds to me like a good deal. Imagine a partnership where you get to keep 90 percent. Then God says, "Test me in this, and see if I don't give you the nations."

Now this was a challenge for me, but I've come around to God's way of thinking. I've gotten in the habit of tithing and trusting in God to deliver on His promises. I've learned the difference between wants and needs. And honestly, since I've learned to tithe, I've never come up short. Our God is a faithful God who anticipates and meets our every need—in His perfect time and after we step out in faith.

Finance from a worldly perspective is another topic. This involves planning, accounting, organizing, partnership, and direction. This is a foreign concept to anyone who grew up in our house. We didn't plan. Our choice came down to the question "Is this good?" and if it was, then we would figure out how to pay for it. We got a lot of our wants met and some very high credit card bills in the process.

I've spent a lot of time trying to figure out how to present this to you. In one version, this topic was seven pages long, and growing. Fortunately, that draft got lost when I changed computers. Then in January of 2015, I took part in one of our church small groups. I took the Dave Ramsey Financial Peace University course. For the first time, everything was presented in one place in a clear and concise step-by-step approach.

The approach is simple (that's right—simple, not easy) but requires a lifetime commitment. Things that I had struggled with for years were right there in front of me in black and white. I knew early in the course that the information was so good at this age that I wished I had had it in my twenties. I really believe that everyone, no matter your age, can benefit from this information.

The dream that God laid on my heart is that this generational curse of poverty, real or perceived, stops here. It ends with me. So to anyone in my family line who has the courage to take control of their finances, now or in the future, I make the following offer.

I will work with you and will pay for your Dave Ramsey Financial Peace University education. I'm that committed to this program.

Thoughts from Aunt Jan and Uncle George

There are many, connected aspects to finance. Hopefully, you earn enough money to spend, save, invest, and create wealth. You'll need to educate yourself and develop your financial skills. Identify areas of finance that interest you, and monitor these areas to build your knowledge.

Start your focus of finances by creating your own budget to learn your spending habits and ultimately help you reach your financial goals. Change your budget when you need to change it; remember, it's your budget, and it's on your side.

Remember, no one cares more about your finances than you do. Your finances can only do one of three things: grow, stay stagnant, or shrink.

Seek knowledge through education and professionals. If you elect to use a financial planner, do not simply go along with their suggestions; ask questions and be involved. Trust and verify. Always understand what you are investing in before you invest.

When you are knowledgeable enough to invest your money in company stocks, never invest more than you are prepared to lose. Investing is simple and complex. The basics do not change (buy low and sell high.) There are many ways to accomplish this, and it's the many ways that make investing complex and difficult. Have a plan B detailing what you will do when your investment has run its course successfully or not.

FINANCE

THE SECRET

Financial Peace University.

OUR GOAL

Live long and prosper.

FRIENDSHIP

"Friends come and friends go, but a true friend sticks
by you like family."

—Proverbs 18:24

There's a childhood round that goes, "Make new friends, but keep the old, one is silver and the other gold." People come and go in our lives, and far too many of our acquaintances think themselves friends. But a true friend is forever. If you can count five true friends in your life, consider yourself lucky.

We make friends in our local environment. In large degree, our mobility determines our selectivity. In the early years, we select our friends at school and from the neighborhood. We are limited by where we can walk or ride our bikes.

Later, we go out of our neighborhood to school, we learn to drive, we get a job, and we expand our surroundings. Our selections now are based less on mobility and more on similar interests. We associate with more people, from different backgrounds and experiences, and we expand the pool of people from which we choose our friends.

Notice I said, "Choose our friends." That's right, don't just let friendship happen. Choose your friends, and choose wisely. I can't say this enough. These are choices you need to make based on your personal character and values. You will rise or sink to the level of your associates. Choose friends who will inspire you to do your best, friends who will laugh with you and cry with you. If you want good friends, you must be a good friend.

Acquaintances will disappear when the going gets rough, but a real friend has your back, like family has your back.

FRIENDSHIP

THE SECRET

People are in our lives for a reason, for a season, or for a lifetime.

THE GOAL

Fill your life with high-quality people.

GOALS

"A life frittered away disgusts God; He loves those who run straight for the finish line."

—Proverbs 15:9

The difference between a goal and a dream is a plan and a timeline.

A successful life doesn't just happen. We need to learn how to make good decisions and choices in our life. We need to set several levels of goals and design plans to achieve those goals.

We need to set immediate, short-term, and long-term goals. Ask yourself questions like, "What do I want to accomplish today? This week? Where do I want to be a month from now, a year from now, five years from now? What do I want my life to say about me?" Once you answer these questions, you can design and implement a plan to reach your goals.

Set the plan in motion, and remain flexible. This plan is not carved in stone but should be written down. Once you write it down, you create a road map. Many roads will lead to the same place. Life can and will take you down many roads with detours. Your personal GPS will recalculate and send you down unexpected routes to arrive at your planned destination. Your personal value system will keep you moving toward your goals.

Thoughts from Aunt Jan and Uncle George

Set yourself short-term, midrange, and long-term goals. You should have goals for every aspect of your life. Review your goals often. Look to the future and plan, dream, and work toward your goals.

Your goals are your road maps for the rest of your life. Don't let life just happen to you; take hold of your life, and drive where you want life to go.

With that said, don't be disappointed when you find yourself off course from time to time; this happens. Instead, find new and better goals. Never stop moving toward your goals.

It is also important to write your goals down as this is what makes them real. When you set goals, make them realistic, challenging, and measurable.

GOALS

THE SECRET

Without a destination, you'll never know when you've arrived.

OUR GOAL

Embrace change. This is God opening a window.

GOVERNMENT * SOCIETY

"When the country is in chaos, everybody has a plan
to fix it. But it takes a leader of real understanding to
straighten things out."

—Proverbs 28:2

Government and society exist in a symbiotic relationship; one cannot exist without the other. Society is a collection of people who share the same values. Government exists at the will and choice of the people to maintain society's values. A civilized society cannot survive without a government committed to maintaining its values and enforcing its laws.

As Americans, our society expresses its values in our Constitution. In order for "we the people" to enjoy the freedoms guaranteed us by our Constitution, we elect legislators who design, debate, customize, and implement laws that we as a society agree to live by. This requires citizen participation.

It is the responsibility of the government to create and maintain an environment in which we the people can thrive, not just simply survive. In our culture, we establish minimum law and insist on maximum compliance. This country was founded on the principle of maximum freedom with minimal government intervention. In fact, our rebellion was against the overbearing policies of large government.

In my opinion, the size of our government has gotten way out of control and intrusive in the lives of a free society. They have overregulated and stifled every area of our lives, from what kind of snacks are in vending machines to the size of our soft drinks; to where we can drill for oil; to open borders; to health care. Our government has tied the hands of our businesses and our professionals with so much government-compliance red tape that our businesses close. This is not the free-market society that our founding fathers envisioned and that I believe in.

I'm a social moderate and a fiscal conservative. I believe that we deserve the freedom to achieve our dreams. At the same time, I believe that as a society we need to take care of the most vulnerable among us. However, our Constitution gives us the right to pursue our happiness, not to stand in line to pick up our welfare checks. Government/Society doesn't owe us a living; it owes us the *right* to earn a living. While we need to create a safety net for those who fall on hard times (we've all been there), it is wrong to create an entitlement society. This is simply a government-supported form of slavery.

If I haven't made it perfectly clear thus far, let me make it clear now: it's the whole "Teach a man to fish" concept. I believe in giving a hand up, not a handout.

I have two fears for my country. My first fear is that we have become so politically correct that we are losing sight of who we are as a society. My second fear is that we are trading our free-enterprise system for socialism.

We are losing our vision, our ability to dream, and our ability to create.

If I were elected president today, tomorrow I would cut government in half. Across the board, every agency and every department in the government would be cut in half. If today you have twelve directors, tomorrow you have six; if today you have six secretaries, tomorrow you have three; if today you have fourteen janitors, tomorrow you have seven; if today you have two senators, tomorrow you have one.

Next, I would simplify taxes. I would establish a standard percentage of tax imposed on everyone on every penny of income. Everyone pays the same percentage on every dime of gross income. Finally, I would limit entitlement programs. Limit the length of time people can receive entitlement benefits and tie benefits to education and work training programs.

Now that we've taken back our government, established a fair tax system, and helped our people in need, we can direct our attention to revitalizing the American dream.

GOVERNMENT * SOCIETY

THE SECRET

Is a return to the fundamentals of our Constitution.

OUR GOAL

To live the dream; live free.

HOLISTIC LIVING

"Dear friend, guard clear thinking and common sense with your life; don't for a minute lose sight of them. They'll keep your soul alive and well, they'll keep you fit and attractive."

—Proverbs 3:21

Holistic living is temple management, and this is the great balancing act.

Temple management is the understanding that your body is home to the Holy Spirit. Start by recognizing that God, in the person of the Holy Spirit, resides within each of us. Our obligation is to welcome the Spirit and to create an environment where we reflect our God to the world around us. This is the balancing act between health, exercise, finance, stress, happiness, love, joy, and spirituality.

Holistic living is about accepting responsibility for your life and achieving success, as you define success, across many areas of life. Holistic living is about doing everything but doing everything in moderation. It's paying attention to everything but not obsessing over anything.

Temple management is about balancing work and relaxation, rest and activity, earning and managing your money, reducing stress through nature, meditation, and spirituality.

While health is a major factor in holistic living, it is not the whole story. If you have been blessed with good health, then temple management is maintaining that health by balancing eating and exercising, and on and on. If you have questionable health, then temple management is about improving your health.

In the big picture, simplify your life, reduce your stress, and enjoy the moment you're in.

Thoughts from Aunt Jan and Uncle George

Exercise is a major element of balance in your life. Keep yourself healthy and strong, and you will "live long and prosper.

Holistic living helps you keep your life in balance. Life is a lot like the waves on the shoreline; it's fluid and constantly changing. That is why you need to keep yourself alert and aware of things that affect you. Schedule your life to be in balance. You are in charge of your life, so make sure you make time for fun, work, family, education, etc. You are in charge; there are no excuses, so make it happen.

HOLISTIC LIVING

THE SECRET

You can have it all; you just can't have it all at the same time.

OUR GOAL

To wholly live and experience this life.

HUMANITIES

"Get wisdom—it's worth more than money; choose
insight over income every time."

—Proverbs 16:16

The humanities, when I started college, I thought was a complete
waste of time. I expected that the research and study of the humanities would take up most of my time and there would be little return
on my investment—a waste of my time. Art, music, literature—how
could that impact my career and my future?

Mark this statement: I was wrong!

The fact is I was right about the 80 percent of my efforts going
into the humanities; I just didn't understand the impact they would
have on my life. I figured out a way to tie much of the effort spent on
humanities into my business studies. I found an appreciation for the
humanities, opening a new dimension in my life.

I respect and appreciate painting, though it doesn't move me
the way craft and architecture and sculpture stimulate me. I think
that's the texture, space, and depth that I relate to. I've learned to read
without a highlighter and cherish that time. Music moves my soul.

Your question was about music, so let's take a look. Each generation presses the limits and develops their own sound. And the older
generation says, "I can't believe they call that music." Our life experiences revolve around our beat, and in later years, our memories are
tied to the music of our day. You'll hear a song and remember that it
was playing when (fill in the blank).

I cross generations in music. It really doesn't matter if it's the big bands of the forties, light rock of the fifties and sixties, or classic rock of the seventies. I've never embraced rap, but gospel or secular, rock or classical, country or revival—I love it. I can spend days wrapped up in one musical show or event after another.

From time to time in my past, I've studied the piano. I don't have a lot of talent, but I do have discipline and timing. If I work long enough and hard enough, I can make it happen, and I can absolutely get lost in the process.

I can't tell you which group did what piece, who put out which album, or which artist performs a specific song the best. Sometimes just hearing a song will set my spirit soaring and the next time it won't move me at all. One song can release a flood of memories. Music sets my mood, puts me in touch with the environment, and moves me to action or relaxation. The music of nature, the wind, the air, the water, the birds, the animals, the trees, and the breeze can be a vacation in the middle of turmoil.

We all move to the beat of our own drummer. You have your own song to sing.

HUMANITIES

THE SECRET

It's all a joyful noise unto the Lord.

OUR GOAL

Don't die with your song still inside you.

HUMOR * FUN

"Mean-spirited slander is heartless; quiet discretion accompanies good sense."

—Proverbs 11:12

Humor is a great tool for managing life. Humor can restore your health, break down barriers, reduce stress, and make difficult situations bearable.

Humor takes many forms. You can find humor in slapstick, stand-up, sitcom, political, satirical, and cartoons. Humor is that reaction that simmers just below whatever situation you find yourself in. It's identifying with and connecting to the silly side of life.

What humor is not is hurtful, abusive, demeaning, or insulting.

Learn to identify and appreciate humor in every situation. Humor will manifest itself in a chuckle, a grin, a sideways glance, or an outright belly laugh. Nothing works better at reducing stress and improving health than a good belly laugh. Immerse yourself in comedy, and learn to laugh out loud. Eventually you'll be able to see the bizarre in most of life's circumstances.

Take what you do seriously, but don't take yourself seriously. Learn to laugh at yourself and laugh at your situation. Learn to find the ridiculous side of life. If you need some help with this, just stand naked in front of a full-length mirror.

God has a great sense of humor, and laughter is a saving grace.

Thoughts from Aunt Jan and Uncle George

Fun is a powerful force allowing your spirits to soar. If you are having difficulty finding fun, smile first and fun will follow. Smiling and having fun is always magnified with others.

Fun, satisfaction, and personal accomplishments go hand in hand. These are the reasons to get up each morning and follow your plans for the day. Fun is the heart of life. Yes, there are times that you need to do things that are not fun, but with the right motivation, you focus, learn, and grow. Always look for fun in what you find yourself doing.

As Mary Poppins says in the song "A Spoon Full of Sugar," "in every job that must be done, there is an element of fun. When you find the fun, snap, the job's a game. And every job you undertake becomes a piece of cake!"

Don't take yourself—or life—too seriously. Relax, smile, and laugh!

H U M O R * F U N

THE SECRET

Life is short, don't forget to laugh.

THE GOAL

Choose to live a joyful life.

LIFE * DEATH *
REINCARNATION

"Take this to heart. Do what I tell you—Live!"
—Proverbs 4:4

Life is a journey, death is a destination, and reincarnation is a do over.

In my head, I accept that this life is an awesome gift, and in my heart, I accept the responsibility to fully embrace, experience, and totally enjoy this life. Some people believe our mission is to live a "holy" life. I believe our mission is to wholly live our life.

Life is like going away to college. Our Father has sent us here on a learning experience. We have each been uniquely designed, tweaked, equipped, and empowered for the mission we've been sent on. Just like college, some of us are on a four-year plan, some on a five-year plan, and some on a ten-or-more-year plan. Some of us live short lives, and some of us are in it for the long haul. Some of us learn quickly, and some take more time. When we complete our degree, we go home.

The good news is God wants us to pass—to make the grade. He gives us lots of do overs. Death is the destination. The Bible makes it very clear that man cannot look on the face of God and live. I think that what happens at the time of death is that we get just a glimpse of the glory of God and it literally takes our breath away.

Again, God wants all His children to come home to Him in heaven. So we get do overs. That's called reincarnation. I believe that we keep coming back until we get it right.

LIFE * DEATH * REINCARNATION

THE SECRET

Find something to live for.

OUR GOAL

To do the best you can, and when you know better, do better.

LOVE

"Don't lose your grip on love and loyalty. Tie them around your neck; carve their initials on your heart. Earn a reputation for living well in God's eyes and the eyes of the people."

—Proverbs 3:3–4

It's really important that you get the difference between love and lust. You know that feeling you get when you first see or meet someone and all the hormones start racing around inside you? You get butterflies in your stomach, and you suddenly hold your stomach in and stand taller. You start fantasizing and assign all your beliefs about love to the person you just met and know absolutely nothing about. You touch, and you get "the fever, the fever that's so hot you burn." That's lust and has everything to do with sex and nothing to do with love.

There is no such thing as love at first sight—love happens over time.

In the love passage, 1 Corinthians 13:4–8, St. Paul writes the following:

"Love is patient, love is kind, love is not jealous, it does not put on airs, it is not snobbish. Love is never rude, it is not self-seeking, it is not prone to anger; neither does it brood over injuries. Love does not rejoice in what is wrong but rejoices with the truth. There is no limit

to love's forbearance, to its trust, its hope, its power to
endure. Love never fails."

I would add that love is a highly charged emotion that strives for good, not evil. Love is active, never passive. Love is passionate and forceful. Love is expansive and inclusive. Love is gentle and soft. Love is unconditional, not dependent on performance. Love is joy and peace.

LOVE

THE SECRET

Love finds you when you least expect it.

THE GOAL

Love is inclusive and expansive. Live, love,
and embrace all that life holds.

MARRIED * SINGLE

"Find a good spouse; find a good life—and even more: the favor of God!"

—Proverbs 18:22

Since the beginning of time, people have been coming together in couples. We call this marriage. We marry for many reasons: companionship, comfort, pleasure, strength, protection, stability, and support, all in the name of love. We are stronger together than when we are alone.

In my opinion, getting married or staying single is a lifestyle choice. I believe there are only two reasons to get married:

1. Because you choose to have children who deserve to be raised in a solid family.
2. You've found a partner who will support and inspire you and who will work with you to achieve all your life dreams and goals.

These are not mutually exclusive concepts, but like all choices in life, you have both positives and negatives to consider.

If you chose to marry, you are taking on a partner for life. You have decided that your character and values match, and your dreams and goals are on the same trajectory. You are not just marrying your partner, you are marrying the value system of the family your partner comes from. You are accepting responsibility for and accountability to your life partner.

This is not the person who is in and out and back into your life. This is the person you expect to spend the next eighty years with. This is the person you choose to weather the storms with. There will be storms. This person is your rudder.

If you choose to marry, the best advice I can give you is to keep open lines of communication in every area of your life, forgive quickly, don't keep score, and don't keep a running account of what you consider to be your partner's faults and failures.

I never found that one special person with matching values and who I would trust with my dreams. That means I am responsible to and accountable only for myself. In some ways, I guess that's easier. In other ways, as a single, I carry the full load alone. I'm not saying that I don't have supportive people in my life. I have a great support system, but I am the only one setting and working to make my dreams come true.

If you choose to remain single, my best advice to you is to identify and work with an accountability partner. This is a person you trust enough to talk over all your life's major decisions with. You still make the decisions, but they get to hold your feet to the fire.

This should be a person who knows your faults and failures and still loves you enough to tell you when you're making a mistake and when you're being a jerk. This is the person who will stand with you no matter what happens or how life comes against you.

Friends will come and go, but family is forever. Start by looking to your parents, then siblings, then extended family—these are the people who will have your back forever.

Thoughts from Aunt Meg

How do you know when to get married? When there's nothing you can think of that you want to do with your life that wouldn't be better with that person at your side, then it's time. How do you stay happily married? Never keep score. On anything. Ever.

MARRIED * SINGLE

THE SECRET

Know who you are, and be true to yourself.

OUR GOAL

Married or single, choose well.

NATURE

"God's blessing makes life rich; nothing we do can improve on God."

—Proverbs 10:22

How unusual for me to talk with you about nature? I think it's great, and should be kept outside. A couple of times a year, I venture out into it. I think part of my problem is confusing nature and weather.

I've just spent seven and a half hours driving north to Grandpa Wayne's cabin, and I'm just overwhelmed with the beauty of nature. Now I respect nature, and I really do love a good rainstorm. I also know that Mother Nature can be a real bitch: snowstorms, freezing weather, tornados, earthquakes—I could go on and on. But then I'm struck by the blazing color of autumn in the north woods, by a sky blue pink sunset over the lake, the soft lapping of the lake up against the pier and the land, when I sit in front of a crackling fire sipping a glass of wine. I find it hard to imagine that anyone could deny the existence of God.

"Be still, and know that I am with you."

I do love the sea—actually, any water. My best vacations have been cruises. I absolutely love sailing. I can completely lose myself just sitting on a pier staring out at a sunset over a lake. Sometimes when I'm in the dentist's chair and I have to escape, I go sailing off Diamond Head. I think the whole sea thing is genetic, going back to Great-Great-Grandfather Angus McIntyre, who was a captain on the Great Lakes.

The sea—that's nature, isn't it?

Thoughts from Aunt Jan and Uncle George

We are all part of this beautiful planet with nature all around us. You might find, like us, that nature holds many answers. These answers come when sitting quietly and contemplating or by observing how nature works.

NATURE

THE SECRET

Nature does not hurry, yet everything is accomplished.

OUR GOAL

Nurture your mind, body, and soul by
taking a walk with Mother Nature.

PATRIOTISM

"Without good direction, people lose their way; the more wise counsel you follow, the better your chances."

—Proverbs 11:14

It's the Fourth of July weekend. The flag is flying. Military bands are playing patriotic songs. Fireworks displays are lighting the sky. We swell with pride as together we celebrate the birth of our nation. That's the expression of our patriotism, but what does it mean to be a patriotic American?

Patriotism is the love of and loyalty to our nation. Patriotism is our belief that our country is superior to all other countries because we were born in it. Patriotism does not mean that we are better than other people, but that we are proud of what we have accomplished as a nation and we have no intention of giving it up.

Beyond simply saluting the flag, patriotism is our pledging allegiance to all that America stands for and the best that we offer to the world. True liberty is living as we should, not as we like.

We celebrate the right to hold ideas that are different and our freedom to think as we please. At the core of who we are, we believe in fairness, equality, freedom, and justice. We are loyal. We love, support, and will defend our country. We understand that freedom and democracy come at a price, and if necessary, we will defend our way of life with our lives.

Patriotism requires action. This is a government of the people, and we must participate in that process. Our disagreements with our government are not grudge fights between parties but more like lovers' quarrels with our fellow citizens. We stay committed to working together to move our country forward.

No one is safe or secure until we are all safe and secure. Our founding fathers and mothers declared their independence. We must declare our interdependence.

PATRIOTISM

THE SECRET

The American dream is still alive and attainable
if you work hard to achieve it.

THE GOAL

To respect the beliefs of others while holding true to our own.

POLITICS

"We don't expect eloquence from fools, nor do we expect lies from our leaders."

—Proverbs 17:7

Some people say it's a game, others say it's the only game. It exists everywhere: work, school, church, government—it's everywhere. I hate politics—or is it just career politicians?

Politics, except for government, is just a word that is interchangeable with organizational behavior. The idea that who you know and how you position yourself is more important than what you know and how you perform is just a fact of life. Observe your environment, join the culture, accept the behavior, or move on. I would suggest an "improv" drama class might be helpful for everyone. Always remember and never forget; it's not your environment to change.

If you're looking for something different, look someplace else, or if you're really into leadership, start your own environment elsewhere. This is America! As long as you don't break the law or destroy what someone else has put in place, you're free to establish your own ideas and culture. Go for it!

Governmental politics is a different story. I would have a hard time encouraging anyone I know to go into politics. I've reached a point where I don't trust anything any of them have to say. I look at what they do, what they accomplish, and what tactics they use to get to where they are.

My personal position is that I believe in the Constitution. I believe in small government, and I'm anti–professional politicians. I consider myself a social moderate (limited support systems) and a fiscal conservative (common sense). And I strongly maintain that these concepts can and do exist in a free-market system.

POLITICS

THE SECRET

Don't bother debating politics with family and friends; you will never change their minds.

OUR GOAL

To elect leaders, not simply managers.

PRAYER

"Fools are headstrong and do what they like; wise people take advice."

—Proverbs 12:15

Prayer is an important part of my life. My day starts and ends with prayer. I strongly believe in the power of prayer. But prayer is only one part of the equation. Prayer without faith and action goes nowhere.

Prayer is our opportunity to have a conversation with God. When we pray, we talk with God. But to have a conversation, at some point, we need to shut up and listen; this is when God talks to us. Stop the monologue and start a dialogue.

Faith believes when everything around you says that's impossible. Faith is the complete opposite of worry. Christ said, "It will be done unto you according to your faith." Prayer without faith is useless.

Prayer and faith won't cut it either. You must add action if you expect results. Pray like only God can make a difference; then work like it's all on your shoulders. You have to step out in faith and act in order for your prayers to be answered. Amen!

Years ago, Anthony asked me, "How do you pray?" Here's an expanded version of my answer. In my opinion, there are three types of prayer: traditional, formal, and conversational. Traditional prayer is like going to Mass. This is a gathering of believers collectively praying the same prayer. Formal prayer is expressing the same thoughts and words in the same sequence over and over, like saying the Hail Mary or the Our Father.

Conversational prayer, my favorite, is walking through life holding a conversation with God. I believe that this is the prayer God is looking for most. He wants to be intimately involved in every area of our lives. Big or small, work or play, majorly important or trivial, God wants to be our best friend. He wants to hang out with us, but you have to invite Him in.

God spoke all things into existence. He spoke it—He called it out—and it's important to pray out loud. Speaking it causes the universal energy to start responding to your intention. Silent prayer is when we shut up and listen. Pray like it has already happened. Believe what you know in your heart, not what you can see with your eyes.

I start my day with prayer. Before my feet touch the floor, while they are still dangling off the side of the bed, I thank God. I pray, "Lord God Almighty, thank you for this day. Thank you for the sun that shines, for the air that I breathe, for my being able to see and to hear. Thank you for this day, and thank you for the grace you've already given me to do this day to meet its challenges, to rise above its negativity, to embrace its opportunities.

"And thank you, Lord, for this strong, healthy, disease-free body that you've given me to live in, to love in, to work in, and to worship in. Despite past abuse and neglect, it continues to function exactly as you designed it to function: strong and healthy and disease-free until the day that you suddenly and unexpectedly call me home. Good morning, Lord."

Now I can get out of bed and get my day started.

I think it's important to seek God in the morning. It's like returning the first fruits of your activities to God. I have my first cup of coffee every morning with the Lord. I worship, I give thanks, I ask His favor, and I invite Him to spend the day with me. And when I go to bed at night, I say good night and thank-you.

PRAYER

THE SECRET

"You have not because you ask not." So pray out loud, pray big and bold prayers, and believe.

THE GOAL

To have an intimate walking and working relationship with God.

RELIGION * FAITH
* SPIRITUALITY

"When the storm is over, there is nothing left of the
wicked; good people, firm on their rock foundation,
aren't even fazed."

—Proverbs 10:25

I believe that each of us is born with a hole inside of us and we spend
our lives trying to fill that hole. We try to fill it with money, work,
people, things, shopping, alcohol, drugs, events, gambling, sex, and
on and on and on.

However, there is only one thing that can fill that hole: God, in
whatever way you perceive him/her. Eventually you'll realize the only
way to achieve contentment is to pursue God. This is spirituality.

Religion, on the other hand, I believe to be a necessary evil—
necessary but evil nonetheless. Organized religion is the well-inten-
tioned answer to a quick fill of that internal hole. It's a set of rules
we must follow in order to be an accepted part of a specific group
(Catholic, Lutheran, Methodist, Jew, Muslim, Baptist, etc.) of believers. But religion is necessary in that it provides a base from which we
begin to ask questions that set us off in varying directions in the pursuit of God, the process of which is the journey to spirituality.

Faith is the process through which we achieve spirituality. As we
work our way through the religious questions, we learn the Word of
God, the Bible. As we expose ourselves to the Word of God, we learn

the promises of the Old Testament and see that they are fulfilled in the New Testament. We see that God is good to His Word and we can trust Him to do what He says He will do.

And spirituality, that's the bonus. To live in the complete knowledge that there is nothing we can do that can add to or improve upon what Christ did for us on the cross. Yet God wants to live in relationship with us. Our Heavenly Father wants to be our best friend. He wants to be involved in every aspect of our lives. He welcomes the time we spend with Him. It is total and complete unconditional love.

RELIGION * FAITH * SPIRITUALITY

THE SECRET

Know that where you are on the journey is
exactly where you're supposed to be.

OUR GOAL

To fully embrace each step along the way
knowing that God is large and in charge.

SAVINGS * INVESTMENTS

"Sloth makes you poor; diligence brings wealth."
—Proverbs 10:4

Let's not confuse these two. Savings is short term, starts with the first dollar you receive, and has a designated purpose. Investments are long term and start after you have a fully funded emergency fund. These are designated for wealth building and long life security.

We can't begin to discuss investments until we have developed the habits of forecasting, budgeting, planning, and saving. Our first goal in saving is to have an emergency fund. This should be three to six months of expenses held in cash with immediate access. Probably the best place for this is something like a money market account. You won't get much interest on this money, but you will have immediate access. The purpose of this money is protection and safety, not wealth building.

After you have your emergency fund in place, learn to save for specific things or goals—that new car, that boat, a sofa, the vacation, or a new TV. By planning, you practice patience, learn deferred gratification, gather information, enjoy the anticipation, redesign the plan, appreciate and make good choices. Once you have your emergency fund and have developed the habit of short-term savings, now we can talk about investments.

Investments are long term. These involve things like owning a home, retirement planning, educational savings, stocks, bonds, mutual funds, and so many more topics. This is where Dave Ramsey put it all together for me. He's the best advice I can give you. So again, let me make this offer to anyone in my family line: I will work with you and pay for your Ramsey education in this area. This is the best advice I can give you. He really makes it simple—not easy, but simple.

There is a third topic here, and it has nothing to do with savings or investments. It's trading. Trading should never be confused with saving or investing. It is a hobby, it's gambling, it's fun and exciting. It's a place where I have spent a lot of time and have had reasonable success. It comes after safety and security.

SAVINGS * INVESTMENTS

THE SECRET

Live for a while like no one else will so you
can live forever like no one else can.

OUR GOAL

To live a secure and reasonably comfortable life.

SCIENCE

"God delights in concealing things; scientists delight in discovering things."

—Proverbs 25:2

I've returned to this page numerous times, and still nothing.

W O W!

Finally!

A topic I have no position or opinion on. I have nothing to say! Ooooooooooooops. Wait. I just had a thought.

There is only so much energy in the world. You can use it up worrying about something or doing something. So stop worrying.

Energy—I think that's science.

SCIENCE

THE SECRET

?

OUR GOAL

?

SERVICE

"It's criminal to ignore a neighbor in need, but compassion for the poor—what a blessing."
—Proverbs 14:21

At the core of being human is the need to give back. The expression "It is better to give than to receive" is based in that human need. Our need to pay it forward with no expectation of reward brings warmth to our inner being. We need to be part of something that is bigger than ourselves. This is service.

Service is putting someone or something before ourselves, and we and the world around us are better for it. Whether our service is part of a group effort or an individual experience, it takes us beyond ourselves. We serve our family, our church, our school, our country, and on and on and on.

It's easy to recognize service when we see group service. We respect and thank our men and women in military uniform for their service to country. When we see strangers pulling together to help people devastated by flood or tornado or earthquake, it's easy to recognize service. We serve when we run a race to raise funds for research. These are easy to recognize.

But remember, he also serves who works behind the scene to support. Serving is helping someone cross the street, singing in the choir, pushing a wheelchair at a nursing home, scooping ice cream, calling bingo, serving food at a shelter, or opening a door for someone struggling with packages. You serve when you help a child tie his shoes or read a book.

We serve best when we help the least able among us. Big or small, this is service. Go beyond yourself, and make a difference.

SERVICE

THE SECRET

The best way to find yourself is to lose yourself in service of others.

THE GOAL

To do what you do so well that others want to join in.

SUCCESS

"Refuse good advice and watch your plans fail; take good counsel and watch them succeed."
—Proverbs 15:22

The world sees success as having the big house, the new car, regular awesome vacations, a great job and the accumulation of money. Look around you. You will find people who have all these things and are still not happy. They are everywhere. This is not success, this is glitz.

Now that we have that out of the way, let's have the more difficult conversation. In your opinion, what is personal success? In my opinion, personal success is living a balanced life. For me, a successful life is a happy, balanced life with enough money to pay my bills, good health, good relationships (first with God and then with all the others in my life), and a happy, healthy family. This requires success across many areas of life. Success is not something you do, it is something you become.

It is vital you establish your own definition of success across many areas. Goals without measurement are simply dreams. Your definition must include reasonable measurements of success. Once you identify your personal success, achievement will follow your definition.

Here, we go back to some decision-making and goal-setting issues. While achievement in any area can be gratifying, let's raise the level of your whole life experience. Achieving goals in one area of life contributes to your total life experience.

The first step to success is to understand who you are and what you stand for. To succeed on the outside, you must first succeed on the inside. Know your own mind, and stay true to yourself.

In defining your personal and financial success, ask yourself what roles money, friends, and happiness play in your life. What about integrity, honesty, values, love, and compassion?

Success is a multifaceted personal concept. By defining what it means to you and by taking the time to write it down, you automatically move your life in the direction of success.

Thoughts from Aunt Jan and Uncle George

You determine your success.

SUCCESS

THE SECRET

Success is not the key to happiness. Happiness is the key to success.

OUR GOAL

To have the courage to try hard again and again and again.

WAR * PEACE

"If you fall to pieces in a crisis, there wasn't much to you in the first place."

—Proverbs 24:10

Sounds like the start of a good novel.

From the beginning of time, human beings have been fighting wars. The first wars were fought face-to-face, and there was no question about who had skin in the battle. Time passed, and war expanded to the sea and ultimately to the sky, and now we add to the mix cyber technology.

As Americans, we have always enjoyed the blessing of distance, and wars were fought on other shores. I prefer to fight these battles before they come knocking at our door. Unfortunately, however, now the war is not just at our door but is sitting in our living rooms. While we are sure what we're fighting, we are not always sure exactly who we are fighting.

Our fathers fought the Nazis. We fought Communism. You will fight Islamic terrorism. Peace has always been and will continue to be the goal.

If the secret to living is finding something to live for, then you must be willing to die to protect it. For me, that's living in the freedom of our American culture—a freedom that many men and women died for. I don't embrace war, but there is such a thing as a justifiable war. When evil rises up among us, we must take it out.

Freedom is not free. Far too often the price of freedom is blood. Freedom demands commitment, vigilance, and citizen participation.

Peace is our goal. We have little control over world peace, but we have a great deal of control over our personal peace. So bloom where you're planted. Take control of your life: choose your friends and acquaintances well, forgive quickly, choose your battles.

Choose your battles. Not every choice or decision you make in life centers around your value system. Ask yourself, "Is this the hill I'm willing to die for?" If you answer yes, then defend your position.

WAR * PEACE

THE SECRET

Identify and confront evil where you find it, and move on.

OUR GOAL

To live with inner personal peace and strive for world peace.

WISDOM

"Above all and before all, do this: Get Wisdom!"
—Proverb 4:8

Wisdom is the accumulation of knowledge and experience that you have on this journey called life. Wisdom is something to aspire to, something that must be acquired. Wisdom cannot be taught or purchased.

Knowledge and wisdom are not the same. Knowledge is learned information whereas wisdom comes through personal experience. Knowledge joined with experience becomes your personal history.

When discernment is added to personal history, it creates wisdom. Discernment is the ability to apply accumulated knowledge and experiences to effectively address problems. When we learn to recognize similarities and patterns in our life, we can avoid repeating errors. Once we learn to separate what is important in life from what is mere distraction, we can channel our energy and focus on our goals and dreams.

Wisdom is the ability to temper our feelings with our experiences. Our feelings often change, but our experiences remain constant. Knowing when to talk and when to listen, knowing when to act, when to wait, and when to do nothing is all part of applied wisdom.

Wisdom is action oriented. Wisdom is the ability to recognize and apply the truth. Wisdom is becoming adept at perceiving what is important in a situation and to routinely act in ways that lead to intended results.

Thoughts from Aunt Jan and Uncle George

Wisdom comes from life experiences. Wisdom can be shared with others; watch and listen to gain wisdom from others. If someone is different, even very different from you, you can learn from them.

Thoughts from Aunt Meg (This bears repeating)

If you're going to make a mistake in life, make it FABULOUSLY. That way, the lesson you learn will stick, and you won't ever have to make that mistake again.

WISDOM

THE SECRET

Knowledge + experience + discernment = wisdom

OUR GOAL

God, grant me the serenity to accept the things I cannot change, the courage to change the things that I can change, and the wisdom to know the difference.

WORK

"The diligent find freedom in their work; the lazy are oppressed by work."

—Proverbs 12:24

Work—thank God for the might of it. Work—thank God for the right of it. There is some deep-down need inside each of us to be productive. Look at Maslow's hierarchy of human needs:

1. Safety (food, shelter, clothing)
2. Security (life and health insurance, savings and investments)
3. Social (interaction with other people)
4. Self-esteem (how we see ourselves in the world)
5. Self-actualization (the achievement of our dreams)

Work answers most of these needs for most people.

For me, work provides structure and accountability. In some respects, it functions as a means of discipline. Because I have to be at work, I have other life demands I'm forced to address (shopping, laundry, house cleaning). Without work, I can manage to ignore or postpone these errands until these little things become overwhelming projects leading to depression.

Now while both a job and a career come under the heading of work, there are major differences. With a job, you typically have the structure of a forty-hour work week. You exchange your time, energy and know-how for a paycheck and sometimes benefits. A job is a means to an end.

A job meets our needs for safety, security, and (to some extent) social interaction, and then you go home. You leave your job behind you and have no additional commitment to the company's future.

With a career, you work open-ended hours; you exchange your time, education, and talent in pursuit of a long-term objective. You never shut down from your future and how it ties to the company. With a career, you'll meet your needs for safety, security, social inter- action, self- esteem, and (to some extent) self-actualization. Your challenge is to keep from having your whole identity wrapped up in what you do.

It's really important that you separate who you are from what you do. You are so much more than your job or career. Don't lose sight of who you are as a person, the human side of your existence.

If you find something you really love to do, you'll never work a day in your life.

Thoughts from Aunt Jan and Uncle George

Love what you do, and it will not feel like work. If you do not enjoy your work, have the courage to move on.

WORK

THE SECRET

Don't lose who you are for your paycheck.

OUR GOAL

To balance life and work.

PART II

Nuggets

"So, my dear friends, listen carefully; those who embrace these my ways are most blessed.
Mark a life of discipline and live wisely; don't squander your precious life.
Blessed the man, blessed the woman, who listens to me, awake and ready for me each morning, alert and responsive as I start my day's work.
When you find me, you find life, real life to say nothing of God's good pleasure but if you wrong me, you damage your very soul; when you reject me, you're flirting with death."

—Proverbs 8:32–36

NUGGETS

Joy is a lifestyle choice; happiness is event related.

Management and leadership are not the same; the goal of management is to maintain the status quo while leadership is visionary and creates.

Forgiveness is accepting that you cannot change the past. Forgiveness is about you and has nothing to do with the other person. Forgiveness allows you to move on.

Reconciliation is putting things back together. Forgiveness and reconciliation are not the same thing.

The journey of a thousand miles starts with one step.

Growing old is not for wimps.

You are only as sick as your deepest and darkest secret.

You can have it all. You just can't have it all at the same time.

Life is not supposed to be easy; it's supposed to be worth it.

Don't waste your pain. Stop asking yourself, "Why is this happening to me?" and start asking, "Why is this happening for me, what's the lesson here?"

Always remember and never forget, it's not how you play the game that counts, it's whether you win or lose.

Whether you think you can or you think you can't, you're right.

Don't sweat the small stuff, and all stuff is small stuff.

The only opinions about you that matter are your own and God's.

There's no rewind—you learn as you go along.

My happiness is not your responsibility, and I am not responsible for your happiness.

Relationships matter; put time and effort into them.

Say yes when you mean yes, no when you mean no, and feel good about it.

I like the person I've become. If you don't, that's your problem.

Choose your battles. Some things just are not worth fighting about.

It's not your job to save the world. Someone already has that job, and He's done a good job.

It's never too late to pursue your dream. It's never too late.

Don't force a long-term solution into a short-time decision.

Stay alert for teachable moments.

Choose happiness.

Getting overly excited about the future is almost disrespectful to today.

Bonding with the right people and things makes you strong so that you are not vulnerable to the things that bring you down.

A command performance requires your presence. There is simply no acceptable excuse for your absence.

Advice comes from a place of love and is meant for your good. You don't have to accept it, but it is foolish to simply disregard or ignore it.

Apply the KISS style of management to your life: keep it simple, stupid.

BENEDICTION
(Rev. Richard Halverson, former chaplain to the US Senate)

You go nowhere by accident.
Wherever you go, God is sending you.
Wherever you are, God has put you there.
God has a purpose in your being there.
Christ lives in you and has something
He wants to do through you where you are.
Believe this and go in the grace and love and power of Jesus Christ.

THE BEGINNING

ABOUT THE AUTHOR

Mary Reinert is thrilled, thankful, and still quite amazed about the publication of her first work, *In Youth We Learn: In Age We Understand*. She was inspired to write by her nephew Anthony, who asked repeatedly then eventually cajoled her for wisdom and life lessons. Mary was further inspired by her late mother, Rita C. Reinert, who enjoyed success as a self-published author in her last decade.

Mary set out to compile a life manual for future generations, sharing hard-won wisdom in hopes that common and painful mistakes will not need to be repeated in their entirety by those who succeed us.

This book was initially intended for her extended family, who happen to number in the hundreds; they are a fertile bunch. On the heels of the enthusiastically positive reception of her initial self-published run, she was pleasantly surprised (shocked, really) to learn that a wider audience clamored for her wisdom.

Happily, for us, she plans to continue writing.

CPSIA information can be obtained
at www.ICGtesting.com
Printed in the USA
BVHW07s2122160518
516408BV00004B/403/P

9 781641 147033